The Power of Persistence Unlocking Your Full Potential and Achieving Goals

Martin Paul

The Power of Persistence Unlocking Your Full Potential and Achieving Goals
Copyright © 2023 by Martin Paul

The first edition was published in 2023

ISBN:

Published by:
Noya
1663 Liberty Drive
Hyderabad, IN 47403
www.noyapublishers.com

This book is self-published using on-demand printing and publishing, which allows it to be printed and distributed globally.

TABLE OF CONTENTS

Chapter 1: The Importance of Persistence

Understanding the Power of Persistence

In the pursuit of our goals, we often encounter obstacles and setbacks that can make us question our abilities and the feasibility of our dreams. However, it is crucial to recognize the power of persistence and its ability to unlock our full potential and help us achieve our goals. In this subchapter, we will delve into the concept of persistence and understand how it can be harnessed to overcome challenges and reach new heights of success.

Persistence is the unwavering commitment to pursuing our goals despite the difficulties we encounter along the way. It is the inner strength that keeps us going, even when the odds seem insurmountable. Understanding the power of persistence requires us to embrace the fact that setbacks and failures are part of the journey to success. Rather than viewing them as roadblocks, we should see them as opportunities for growth and learning.

One key aspect of persistence is having a clear vision and unwavering belief in our goals. When we have a strong sense of purpose, it becomes easier to stay motivated and push through obstacles. By reminding ourselves of why we started in the first place, we can maintain focus and persevere even when the going gets tough.

Another crucial element of persistence is developing resilience. Resilience allows us to bounce back from failures and setbacks, learning from our mistakes and adapting our strategies accordingly. It is the ability to keep going when others might give up, knowing that success often comes to those who persist and never lose sight of their dreams.

One of the most valuable lessons in understanding the power of persistence is realizing that success is rarely achieved overnight. It requires consistent effort, determination, and a willingness to keep trying even when progress seems slow. By embracing the long-term mindset, we can break down our goals into smaller, more manageable steps and celebrate each milestone along the way.

In conclusion, understanding the power of persistence is essential for anyone looking to achieve their goals. By recognizing that setbacks are part of the journey, maintaining a clear vision, developing resilience, and embracing a long-term mindset, we can unlock our full potential and overcome any obstacles that come our way. Remember, success rarely comes to those who give up too soon – it comes to those who persist and persevere in the face of adversity.

Overcoming Obstacles in Pursuit of Goals

In the journey towards achieving our goals, obstacles often arise unexpectedly. These obstacles can be discouraging, demotivating, and sometimes even cause us to doubt our abilities. However, it is important to remember that obstacles are not roadblocks but rather opportunities for growth and self-improvement. In this subchapter, we will explore effective strategies to overcome obstacles and stay focused on the path to success.

The first step in overcoming obstacles is to develop a positive mindset. Instead of viewing obstacles as setbacks, see them as challenges that can be conquered. Embrace a growth mindset, understanding that obstacles are essential for personal development and the achievement of your goals. Remember, every successful person has faced obstacles along their journey; it is how they handled them that made the difference.

Next, it is crucial to break down your goals into smaller, manageable tasks. By doing so, you can tackle one obstacle at a time, making it less overwhelming. This approach allows you to develop a clear plan of action and maintain focus, even when faced with challenges. Celebrate each small victory along the way, as it will keep you motivated and build momentum towards your ultimate goal.

Seeking support is another essential aspect of overcoming obstacles. Surround yourself with like-minded individuals who share your aspirations and can offer guidance and encouragement when you face hurdles. Joining support groups, attending workshops, or finding a mentor can provide valuable insights and help you stay motivated during challenging times.

Additionally, maintaining a flexible mindset is vital. Often, obstacles require us to adjust our plans or find alternative solutions. Embrace change and adapt to unforeseen circumstances, as rigidity can hinder progress. Remember, it is not about how many times you fall down, but how many times you get back up and keep moving forward.

Lastly, self-care is crucial when facing obstacles. Take care of your physical, emotional, and mental well-being. Engage in activities that recharge you, such as exercise, meditation, or spending time with loved ones. Taking care of yourself will enhance your resilience and ability to overcome obstacles with grace and determination.

In conclusion, obstacles are an inevitable part of the journey towards achieving our goals. By adopting a positive mindset, breaking down goals, seeking support, staying flexible, and practicing self-care, we can overcome any obstacle that comes our way. Remember, the power to achieve your goals lies within you – embrace obstacles as opportunities for growth and keep persisting towards your dreams.

Embracing a Growth Mindset for Resilience

In the pursuit of achieving our goals, one of the most powerful tools we can cultivate is a growth mindset. A growth mindset is the belief that our abilities and talents can be developed through dedication, hard work, and perseverance. It is the understanding that failure and setbacks are not indications of our limitations, but rather opportunities for growth and learning.

Resilience is the ability to bounce back from adversity and maintain our determination in the face of challenges. By embracing a growth mindset, we can enhance our resilience and increase our chances of achieving our goals.

When we adopt a growth mindset, we view obstacles and setbacks as temporary roadblocks rather than insurmountable barriers. We understand that setbacks are a natural part of the journey towards success and that they offer valuable lessons and opportunities for growth. Instead of giving up when faced with adversity, we persist and find alternative solutions to overcome the challenges.

A growth mindset also allows us to see failures as stepping stones to success. Rather than being discouraged by failures, we see them as opportunities to learn, adapt, and improve. By reframing our perspective on failure, we can extract valuable insights that can guide our future actions and lead us closer to our goals.

Additionally, a growth mindset encourages us to embrace discomfort and step outside of our comfort zones. We understand that true growth and progress come from pushing ourselves beyond our perceived limits. By challenging ourselves and seeking new experiences, we expand our skills, knowledge, and capabilities, ultimately increasing our chances of achieving our goals.

To embrace a growth mindset for resilience, it is crucial to cultivate self-awareness and self-compassion. We must recognize our fixed beliefs and negative self-talk, replacing them with positive affirmations and a belief in our ability to grow and adapt. Self-compassion allows us to acknowledge our mistakes and setbacks without self-judgment, nurturing a mindset of continuous improvement.

In conclusion, adopting a growth mindset is a powerful tool for resilience in the pursuit of our goals. By embracing challenges, failures, and discomfort as opportunities for growth, we can cultivate the determination and perseverance necessary to overcome obstacles and achieve our full potential. Through self-awareness and self-compassion, we can develop a mindset that empowers us to persist, adapt, and thrive on our journey towards success.

Chapter 2: Setting Clear and Attainable Goals

Identifying Your Core Values and Passions

In the pursuit of achieving our goals, it is essential to have a clear understanding of our core values and passions. These guiding principles serve as a compass, helping us navigate through life's challenges and make decisions that align with our true selves. They provide us with a sense of purpose and drive, propelling us towards success and fulfillment. In this subchapter, we will explore the significance of identifying our core values and passions and how they can contribute to our journey of achieving goals.

To begin with, core values are the fundamental beliefs and principles that define who we are as individuals. They represent our highest priorities and shape our thoughts, behaviors, and actions. Identifying our core values allows us to align our goals and aspirations with what truly matters to us. By doing so, we create a sense of congruence and authenticity, ensuring that our pursuits are in harmony with our innermost desires.

Passions, on the other hand, are the activities or interests that ignite a fire within us. They are the things that bring us joy, fulfillment, and a deep sense of purpose. Identifying our passions is crucial because they become the driving force behind our goals. When we are passionate about something, we are more likely to persist through challenges and setbacks, ultimately leading us to achieve our desired outcomes.

So how can we identify our core values and passions? It starts with introspection and self-reflection. Take the time to evaluate what truly matters to you in life. What principles do you hold dear? What activities or interests bring you the most joy and fulfillment? Pay attention to moments when you feel alive and fully engaged, as these can provide valuable insights into your passions.

Additionally, consider seeking feedback from those closest to you. Sometimes, others can recognize our core values and passions more clearly than we can ourselves. Engage in meaningful conversations with friends, family, and mentors who can offer valuable perspectives and insights.

Once you have identified your core values and passions, it is important to integrate them into your goal-setting process. Ensure that your goals are aligned with your values and fueled by your passions. This alignment will provide you with the motivation and resilience needed to overcome obstacles and persevere.

In conclusion, understanding your core values and passions is a crucial step in achieving your goals. By identifying what truly matters to you and what ignites your soul, you can create a path that aligns with your authentic self. This alignment will fuel your motivation, persistence, and ultimately lead you to unlock your full potential and achieve your goals.

Creating SMART Goals for Success

In order to achieve our goals and unlock our full potential, it is crucial to set clear and actionable objectives. SMART goals provide us with a framework that helps us define and attain our aspirations effectively. Whether you are a student, a professional, or simply someone with a burning desire to achieve success, understanding the principles of SMART goals is vital.

SMART goals are Specific, Measurable, Achievable, Relevant, and Time-bound. Let's break down each element and explore how they contribute to your success.

Firstly, specific goals are well-defined and clear. Instead of saying, "I want to be successful," specify what success means to you. This could be earning a specific amount of money, obtaining a particular job title, or starting your own business. The more precise your goal, the easier it becomes to create an action plan.

Next, measurable goals allow you to track your progress and determine whether you are moving in the right direction. For instance, if your goal is to lose weight, set a measurable target such as losing 10 pounds in two months. By monitoring your progress regularly, you can make adjustments to your strategy if needed.

Achievable goals are realistic and attainable. While it is important to dream big, setting goals that are within reach increases your motivation and likelihood of success. Consider your resources, skills, and limitations when setting achievable goals. Remember, it is better to set smaller milestones and celebrate your accomplishments along the way than to set an unrealistic goal and become discouraged.

Relevant goals align with your values and aspirations. Ask yourself, "Why is this goal important to me?" When your goals are meaningful and relevant, you are more likely to stay committed and overcome obstacles. Ensure that your goals resonate with your long-term vision and contribute to your personal growth.

Lastly, time-bound goals have a deadline or target date. Without a sense of urgency, it is easy to procrastinate and lose momentum. Set a specific date by which you want to achieve your goal, and break it down into smaller timeframes to stay on track.

Creating SMART goals is a powerful tool that can transform your life and help you achieve your aspirations. By setting specific, measurable, achievable, relevant, and time-bound objectives, you are giving yourself a roadmap to success. Remember, persistence is key in reaching your goals. Stay focused, remain resilient, and celebrate every milestone along the way. You have the power to unlock your full potential and achieve greatness.

Breaking Down Goals into Manageable Steps

Achieving goals can often feel overwhelming, especially when they seem distant and unattainable. Many individuals struggle to make progress and ultimately give up on their dreams. However, the key to success lies in breaking down goals into manageable steps. By doing so, we can navigate our journey towards success with clarity, focus, and persistence.

The first step in breaking down goals is to clearly define what we want to achieve. Whether it is a career aspiration, a personal milestone, or a health goal, it is essential to have a crystal-clear vision of what we want to accomplish. This clarity will serve as our compass throughout the journey, helping us stay on track and motivated.

Once we have a well-defined goal, the next step is to break it down into smaller, more manageable steps. Think of these steps as milestones along the way, each one bringing us closer to our ultimate objective. Breaking down goals helps to eliminate the overwhelm and makes the entire process more approachable.

It is crucial to set realistic and achievable deadlines for each step. By doing so, we create a sense of urgency and hold ourselves accountable for making progress. These deadlines act as checkpoints, allowing us to evaluate our progress and make any necessary adjustments to our plan.

Furthermore, it is vital to prioritize our steps. Not all tasks are created equal, and some may have a more significant impact on our overall progress. By identifying the most critical steps, we can focus our time and energy where it matters most, making the most efficient use of our resources.

In addition to breaking down goals, it is essential to celebrate each milestone achieved. Celebrating small wins along the way boosts our motivation and reinforces our belief in our ability to succeed. Remember, success is not just the end result; it is also the journey itself.

Finally, remain flexible and adaptable. While breaking down goals into manageable steps provides structure, life is unpredictable, and circumstances may change. It is crucial to be open to adjusting our plans as needed, while still staying focused on our ultimate vision.

In conclusion, breaking down goals into manageable steps is the key to achieving success. By defining our goals, breaking them down into smaller tasks, setting realistic deadlines, prioritizing our steps, celebrating milestones, and remaining adaptable, we can unlock our full potential and make our dreams a reality. So, let us embrace the power of persistence and take those crucial first steps towards achieving our goals.

Chapter 3: Developing a Positive Mindset for Success

Cultivating a Positive Attitude

In the journey of achieving our goals, one of the most crucial factors that determines our success is our attitude. A positive attitude can work wonders and propel us forward, while a negative mindset can hinder our progress and hold us back. In this subchapter, we will explore the power of cultivating a positive attitude and its impact on achieving our goals.

First and foremost, it is important to understand that a positive attitude is not simply about being optimistic or ignoring challenges. Rather, it is about having a mindset that embraces challenges as opportunities for growth and learning. When we approach our goals with a positive attitude, we are more likely to stay motivated, persevere through obstacles, and find creative solutions to problems.

One key aspect of cultivating a positive attitude is practicing gratitude. By focusing on the things we are grateful for, we shift our perspective from what is lacking to what we already have. This mindset of abundance allows us to appreciate the present moment and fuel our motivation to achieve more.

Another important element is self-belief. Developing a strong belief in ourselves and our abilities is crucial for overcoming self-doubt and maintaining a positive attitude. When we believe in our potential, we become more resilient in the face of setbacks and are better equipped to handle challenges that come our way.

Additionally, surrounding ourselves with positive influences and like-minded individuals can significantly impact our attitude. By associating with individuals who share our goals and vision, we create a support system that uplifts and encourages us. The power of positive relationships cannot be underestimated, as they provide us with the necessary motivation and inspiration to keep going.

Finally, practicing self-care and self-reflection is vital for maintaining a positive attitude. Taking time for ourselves, engaging in activities that bring us joy, and nurturing our physical and mental well-being all contribute to a positive mindset. Regular self-reflection allows us to identify and address any negative thought patterns or limiting beliefs that may be hindering our progress.

In conclusion, cultivating a positive attitude is an essential aspect of achieving our goals. By practicing gratitude, fostering self-belief, surrounding ourselves with positive influences, and prioritizing self-care, we can unlock our full potential and overcome any challenges that come our way. With a positive attitude, we have the power to persist and achieve greatness in all areas of our lives.

Overcoming Self-Doubt and Fear of Failure

In our journey towards achieving our goals, self-doubt and fear of failure often stand as formidable barriers. These negative emotions can cripple our progress, leaving us feeling stuck and unable to move forward. However, it is important to remember that self-doubt and fear are not insurmountable obstacles. With the right mindset and tools, we can conquer these challenges and unlock our full potential.

One of the first steps towards overcoming self-doubt and fear of failure is to recognize and acknowledge these emotions. We must understand that it is perfectly normal to experience self-doubt and fear when embarking on a new endeavor. However, it is crucial not to let these emotions define us or dictate our actions. Instead, we should view them as opportunities for growth and self-improvement.

To overcome self-doubt, it is essential to cultivate a positive mindset. Surround yourself with supportive and encouraging individuals who believe in your abilities. Engage in positive self-talk and remind yourself of past successes and achievements. Celebrate small victories along the way, as they serve as a reminder of your capabilities.

Fear of failure often stems from a deep-rooted fear of judgment and rejection. To overcome this fear, it is important to shift our perspective on failure. Instead of viewing it as a negative outcome, we should see failure as a stepping stone towards success. Embrace failure as a valuable learning experience and an opportunity to grow stronger and wiser. Remember, even the most successful individuals have encountered failure on their journey.

Another effective strategy for overcoming self-doubt and fear of failure is to break down our goals into manageable steps. By setting smaller, achievable milestones, we can build momentum and gain confidence in our abilities. Celebrate each milestone reached, and use it as motivation to continue moving forward.

Visualization and positive affirmations are powerful techniques that can help overcome self-doubt and fear. Take a few moments each day to visualize yourself successfully achieving your goals. Imagine how it feels to accomplish what you have set out to do. Repeat positive affirmations such as "I am capable," "I am deserving of success," and "I am fearless." These affirmations will help reprogram your subconscious mind and reinforce a positive mindset.

In conclusion, self-doubt and fear of failure are natural emotions that can hinder our progress towards achieving goals. However, with the right mindset and strategies, we can overcome these obstacles. By acknowledging our emotions, cultivating a positive mindset, embracing failure as a learning opportunity, setting achievable milestones, and utilizing visualization and positive affirmations, we can unlock our full potential and achieve our goals. Remember, you have the power within you to overcome self-doubt and fear, so embrace the journey and persist in your pursuit of success.

Practicing Self-Compassion and Self-Belief

In the journey of achieving our goals, we often face obstacles and setbacks that can leave us feeling discouraged and doubtful. However, the key to unlocking our full potential lies in practicing self-compassion and self-belief. These two powerful tools can help us overcome challenges, stay motivated, and ultimately achieve our goals.

Self-compassion is the practice of treating ourselves with kindness, understanding, and acceptance, especially during difficult times. It involves acknowledging our failures and setbacks without judgement, and instead, offering ourselves love and support. By cultivating self-compassion, we create a safe space within ourselves where we can process our emotions, learn from our mistakes, and grow stronger.

One way to practice self-compassion is through self-care. Taking time to prioritize our physical, mental, and emotional well-being is crucial for maintaining resilience and perseverance. This can involve activities such as exercise, meditation, journaling, or spending quality time with loved ones. By nurturing ourselves, we replenish our energy and build the inner strength needed to overcome obstacles on our path to achieving our goals.

Equally important is cultivating self-belief. Believing in ourselves and our abilities is essential for staying motivated and pushing through challenging times. When we have confidence in our skills and potential, we are more likely to take risks, persist in the face of adversity, and achieve our goals.

To build self-belief, it is crucial to recognize our past accomplishments and strengths. Reflecting on times when we have overcome challenges or achieved success can remind us of our capabilities and fuel our motivation. Surrounding ourselves with positive and supportive individuals can also boost our self-belief. Having a network of people who believe in us can provide the encouragement and validation needed to maintain our self-confidence.

In addition, setting realistic and achievable goals can help us build self-belief. By breaking our larger goals into smaller, manageable tasks, we can experience frequent successes along the way. Each accomplishment serves as evidence of our abilities, reinforcing our self-belief and propelling us forward.

Practicing self-compassion and self-belief are essential components in the journey of achieving our goals. By treating ourselves with kindness and believing in our potential, we create a solid foundation for resilience, motivation, and ultimate success. So, let us embrace these powerful tools, unlock our full potential, and embark on a path towards achieving our goals with unwavering determination. Remember, you are capable, deserving, and worthy of the success you seek.

Chapter 4: Building a Solid Action Plan

Prioritizing Tasks and Managing Time Effectively

In our fast-paced world, it is essential to have the ability to prioritize tasks and manage time effectively in order to achieve our goals. This subchapter will provide you with practical strategies and techniques to enhance your productivity, reduce stress, and ultimately unlock your full potential.

First and foremost, it is crucial to identify your goals. What do you want to achieve? By clearly defining your objectives, you can align your tasks accordingly, ensuring that you stay focused and motivated throughout the process. Make sure your goals are specific, measurable, attainable, relevant, and time-bound (SMART goals). This will enable you to break them down into smaller, more manageable tasks.

Once you have established your goals, it is time to prioritize your tasks. Start by creating a to-do list, either on paper or using digital tools. Determine which tasks are urgent and important, and tackle those first. Avoid getting caught up in trivial or low-priority tasks that can eat up your precious time. By focusing on what matters most, you will make significant progress towards your goals.

Another effective technique for managing time is the Pomodoro Technique. This method involves breaking your work into 25-minute intervals, called pomodoros, with short breaks in between. This structure helps you maintain focus and prevents burnout. Set a timer, work on a task for 25 minutes, and then take a 5-minute break. After completing four pomodoros, reward yourself with a longer break. This technique enhances productivity and ensures that you make steady progress on your goals.

Furthermore, delegation is a valuable skill to develop. Recognize that you cannot do everything yourself, and it is okay to ask for help. Delegate tasks that can be handled by others, freeing up your time for more important responsibilities. Delegation not only reduces your workload but also empowers others to contribute to the achievement of your goals.

Lastly, it is essential to maintain a healthy work-life balance. Dedicate time for self-care, relaxation, and spending quality time with loved ones. Remember, achieving goals is a journey, and it requires consistency and persistence. Taking care of your physical and mental well-being will ensure that you stay motivated and energized throughout the process.

In conclusion, by prioritizing tasks and managing time effectively, you can unlock your full potential and achieve your goals. Identify your objectives, prioritize tasks, use effective time management techniques such as the Pomodoro Technique, delegate when necessary, and maintain a healthy work-life balance. With these strategies in place, you will be well on your way to realizing your dreams and aspirations.

Harnessing the Power of Visualization and Affirmations

In our journey towards success and achieving our goals, it is essential to understand the incredible power of visualization and affirmations. These two techniques, when combined, can help us unlock our full potential and manifest our dreams into reality. Whether you are a student aiming for academic excellence, an entrepreneur striving for business success, or simply someone looking to improve different aspects of your life, mastering the art of visualization and affirmations can be a game-changer.

Visualization is the process of creating vivid mental images of our desired outcomes. It involves using our imagination to see ourselves already achieving our goals, experiencing the emotions that accompany our achievements, and immersing ourselves in the details of our desired reality. By consistently visualizing our goals, we send a powerful message to our subconscious mind, which then starts working towards making our visualizations a reality.

Affirmations, on the other hand, are positive statements that we repeat to ourselves regularly. These statements are designed to reinforce our beliefs, shift our mindset, and cultivate a positive attitude towards our goals. Affirmations serve as powerful reminders of our capabilities, strengths, and the possibilities that lie ahead. By repeating affirmations with conviction and belief, we reprogram our subconscious mind to align with our goals and attract the opportunities and resources necessary for success.

When combined, visualization and affirmations create a potent force that propels us towards our desired outcomes.

By visualizing our goals and affirming them with positive statements, we create a clear vision of what we want to achieve and align our thoughts, emotions, and actions with that vision. This alignment increases our focus, motivation, and determination, leading to enhanced performance and ultimately, the achievement of our goals.

To harness the power of visualization and affirmations effectively, consistency is key. Dedicate regular time each day to practice both techniques. Find a quiet space where you can comfortably visualize your desired outcomes and repeat your affirmations out loud. Be specific in your visualizations and choose affirmations that resonate with you personally. Visualize not only the end result but also the steps you need to take to get there, as this will help you identify and seize opportunities that align with your goals.

In conclusion, by harnessing the power of visualization and affirmations, you can unlock your full potential and achieve your goals. These techniques enable you to create a clear vision, align your thoughts and actions with that vision, and attract the necessary resources and opportunities for success. Embrace the power of visualization and affirmations, and watch as your dreams turn into reality. Remember, persistence is key, so keep visualizing, affirming, and taking inspired action towards your goals, and success will be within your grasp.

Seeking Accountability and Support

In our journey towards achieving our goals, it is essential to recognize the power of seeking accountability and support. While personal determination and self-motivation are crucial, we must acknowledge that we cannot always do everything alone. Connecting with others who can provide guidance, encouragement, and a sense of accountability can significantly boost our chances of success.

Accountability plays a vital role in goal achievement. When we make our intentions known to someone else, we create a sense of responsibility to follow through on our commitments. Sharing our goals with a trusted friend, family member, or mentor helps us stay focused and committed, even when faced with obstacles or distractions. This external accountability provides the necessary push to keep us on track, ensuring that we stay motivated and dedicated to our ultimate aspirations.

Moreover, seeking support from others can provide valuable insights and perspectives. Surrounding ourselves with like-minded individuals, who have similar goals or have already achieved what we aspire to, can inspire us and fuel our determination. Engaging in conversations with these individuals allows us to learn from their experiences, gain new ideas, and discover strategies that have proven successful. Their support and guidance can help us navigate challenges and avoid potential pitfalls, saving us time and effort along the way.

In addition to accountability and guidance, seeking support also fosters a sense of belonging and community.

Connecting with others who are on a similar path not only provides motivation but also creates an environment of understanding. Sharing our struggles, fears, and successes with a supportive community allows us to celebrate wins together, as well as find solace and encouragement during difficult times. This sense of shared experience can be a powerful source of motivation and resilience, reminding us that we are not alone in our pursuit of achieving goals.

To seek accountability and support, it is crucial to actively engage with others who can provide guidance and encouragement. Joining goal-oriented communities, attending seminars and workshops, or seeking out a mentor are excellent starting points. Additionally, technology has made it easier than ever to connect with like-minded individuals through online forums, social media groups, and specialized applications.

In conclusion, seeking accountability and support is an essential component of achieving our goals. By sharing our intentions, seeking guidance, and connecting with others on a similar path, we enhance our chances of success. Accountability keeps us focused, support provides us with valuable insights, and a community of like-minded individuals provides the motivation and resilience needed to reach our full potential. Embracing accountability and support is a powerful step towards unlocking our true potential and realizing our dreams.

Chapter 5: Persevering in the Face of Challenges

Understanding the Nature of Setbacks and Failures

In our journey to achieve our goals, setbacks and failures are inevitable. They can be disheartening, demotivating, and make us question our abilities and aspirations. However, it is crucial to understand that setbacks and failures are not signs of weakness or incompetence; they are an integral part of the path to success. In this subchapter, we will delve into the nature of setbacks and failures, unraveling the valuable lessons they hold and how they can propel us forward on our quest to achieve our goals.

Firstly, setbacks and failures are not permanent. They are temporary roadblocks that provide valuable insights and opportunities for growth. When faced with a setback or failure, it is essential to approach it with a growth mindset. Instead of dwelling on the disappointment, we should focus on what we can learn from the experience. Each setback presents an opportunity to reflect, reassess, and improve our strategies. By embracing setbacks, we can uncover hidden strengths, discover new perspectives, and ultimately become more resilient.

Secondly, setbacks and failures are not indicative of our worth or potential. It is crucial to separate our self-worth from the outcome of our endeavors. Just because we experience a setback does not mean we are incapable or undeserving of success. It merely means that we need to refine our approach or acquire additional skills. By understanding that setbacks are part of the learning curve, we can maintain a positive self-image and continue pursuing our goals with renewed determination.

Thirdly, setbacks and failures often serve as a catalyst for innovation and creativity. When faced with a roadblock, we are forced to think outside the box and explore alternative solutions. These challenges can push us to tap into our creative potential and come up with innovative approaches we may not have considered otherwise. By embracing setbacks as opportunities for growth and innovation, we can transform failures into stepping stones towards success.

In conclusion, setbacks and failures are not the end of our journey towards achieving our goals; they are stepping stones on the path to success. By understanding their nature and embracing them as valuable learning experiences, we can unlock our full potential. Setbacks provide us with opportunities to grow, reflect, and refine our strategies. They do not define our worth or potential, and they often ignite our creativity and innovation. So, the next time you encounter a setback or failure, remember that it is not the end, but rather an opportunity for growth and a step forward on your journey to achieving your goals.

Developing Resilience and Grit

In the pursuit of our goals, we often encounter obstacles, setbacks, and failures that can leave us feeling discouraged and ready to give up. However, it is during these challenging moments that developing resilience and grit becomes crucial. Resilience and grit are the key ingredients that enable us to stay focused, persevere, and ultimately achieve our goals.

Resilience can be defined as the ability to bounce back from adversity, while grit refers to the determination and passion to continue working towards our goals, even when faced with obstacles. Both are essential qualities that can be cultivated and strengthened over time.

One of the first steps in developing resilience and grit is to adopt a growth mindset. This mindset recognizes that failures and setbacks are learning opportunities rather than indications of inherent limitations. By reframing our perspective, we can see setbacks as stepping stones towards success, rather than roadblocks that stop us in our tracks.

Another important aspect is building a support system. Surrounding ourselves with positive, like-minded individuals who encourage and uplift us can have a significant impact on our ability to bounce back from setbacks. These individuals can provide valuable insights, advice, and emotional support during challenging times.

Cultivating self-compassion is also crucial in developing resilience and grit. It is essential to treat ourselves with kindness and understanding when we face setbacks or failures. By acknowledging our efforts and progress, even in the face of adversity, we can build the resilience needed to keep moving forward.

Additionally, setting realistic goals and breaking them down into smaller, manageable steps can help us stay motivated and focused. Celebrating small victories along the way can boost our confidence and reinforce our determination to continue pushing forward.

Lastly, practicing perseverance is a fundamental aspect of developing resilience and grit. It requires discipline and a willingness to keep going, even when the going gets tough. Embracing challenges as opportunities for growth and recognizing that success often requires persistence can help us stay committed to achieving our goals.

In conclusion, developing resilience and grit is essential for anyone striving to achieve their goals. By adopting a growth mindset, building a support system, cultivating self-compassion, setting realistic goals, and practicing perseverance, we can overcome obstacles and setbacks on our path to success. With resilience and grit, we unlock our full potential and become unstoppable in achieving our goals.

Learning from Mistakes and Adapting Strategies

Mistakes are an inevitable part of the journey towards achieving our goals. They are not something to be feared or avoided, but rather embraced as valuable opportunities for growth and improvement. In the quest to unlock our full potential and achieve our goals, it is crucial to understand the power of learning from mistakes and adapting our strategies accordingly.

When we make mistakes, it is essential to resist the temptation to dwell on them or let them define us. Instead, we should view them as valuable lessons and stepping stones towards success. Each mistake holds within it a wealth of knowledge and insights that can guide us towards developing smarter strategies and making better decisions in the future.

One of the keys to learning from mistakes is adopting a growth mindset. This mindset acknowledges that abilities and intelligence can be developed through dedication and hard work. With a growth mindset, we understand that setbacks are not permanent failures but temporary roadblocks that can be overcome with perseverance and resilience. By embracing a growth mindset, we can approach mistakes with a sense of curiosity and a desire to learn.

Adapting our strategies is another essential aspect of achieving our goals. As we encounter obstacles and setbacks, it is crucial to evaluate our current approach and make necessary adjustments. This might involve seeking feedback from mentors or trusted individuals who can provide valuable insights and perspectives. It could also mean exploring alternative methods or considering different approaches to the challenges we face.

Adaptability is a trait that successful individuals possess. They understand that rigidly sticking to one strategy, even if it is not yielding the desired results, is counterproductive. By being open to change and adaptable in our strategies, we can navigate the ever-changing landscape of goal achievement more effectively.

In conclusion, learning from mistakes and adapting strategies are integral components of any journey towards achieving goals. Mistakes should be embraced as valuable learning opportunities, and a growth mindset should be cultivated to foster resilience and perseverance. Adapting strategies involves evaluating our approaches, seeking feedback, and being open to change. By harnessing the power of learning from mistakes and being adaptable, we can unlock our full potential and achieve even the loftiest of goals.

Chapter 6: Maintaining Motivation and Momentum

Celebrating Milestones and Small Victories

In our journey towards achieving our goals, it is crucial to acknowledge and celebrate every milestone and small victory along the way. These moments of triumph not only serve as motivation to keep pushing forward, but they also offer an opportunity to reflect on our progress and appreciate the hard work we have put in.

Often, we are so focused on the end goal that we forget to recognize the smaller achievements that pave the way towards success. By taking the time to celebrate these milestones, we are reinforcing positive habits and instilling a sense of achievement within ourselves. It acts as a reminder that we are capable of overcoming challenges and progressing towards our ultimate aspirations.

Celebrating milestones and small victories also enhances our self-confidence and self-belief. Each step forward serves as evidence that we are making progress and that our efforts are yielding results. This boosts our morale and fuels our determination to persist even when faced with obstacles or setbacks.

Moreover, recognizing these moments of success provides an opportunity for gratitude. It allows us to express appreciation for the support we have received, whether it be from friends, family, or mentors. Gratitude not only strengthens our relationships but also fosters a positive mindset, enabling us to approach future challenges with optimism and resilience.

To effectively celebrate milestones and small victories, it is essential to establish a personal reward system. This can be as simple as treating ourselves to a favorite meal, indulging in a leisure activity, or taking a break to relax and recharge. By associating these rewards with our achievements, we create positive reinforcement that encourages us to continue our pursuit of success.

Furthermore, sharing our milestones and victories with others can be incredibly empowering. Not only does it inspire and motivate those around us, but it also allows us to build a support network that celebrates our wins alongside us. This network can provide valuable encouragement during difficult times and help us stay accountable to our goals.

In conclusion, celebrating milestones and small victories is an essential aspect of achieving our goals. By recognizing our progress, fostering gratitude, and establishing a reward system, we can cultivate a positive mindset and persist in our pursuit of success. So, let us not overlook these significant moments and instead embrace them as stepping stones towards unlocking our full potential.

Staying Inspired and Focused on the End Goal

In our journey towards achieving our goals, it is natural to encounter obstacles and challenges that may test our resolve. It is during these moments that we need to stay inspired and focused on the end goal. This subchapter aims to provide valuable insights and strategies to help you maintain your motivation and drive throughout your goal-achieving journey.

One of the first steps towards staying inspired is to clearly define your end goal. Setting a specific and measurable objective provides you with a clear target to work towards. Without a clear destination in mind, it becomes easy to lose focus and motivation. By defining your end goal, you create a mental image of what you want to achieve, making it easier to stay inspired and focused.

Another effective strategy is to break down your goal into smaller, manageable tasks. This approach allows you to track your progress and celebrate small victories along the way. By accomplishing these smaller tasks, you create a positive feedback loop that boosts your motivation and keeps you inspired to move forward.

It is also important to surround yourself with inspiration. This can be done by seeking out role models who have achieved similar goals or by immersing yourself in books, articles, or videos that align with your aspirations. By exposing yourself to success stories and positive influences, you will find it easier to stay motivated and focused on your own journey.

Additionally, maintaining a positive mindset is crucial in staying inspired. Practice self-affirmations and visualize yourself achieving your goals. Remind yourself of the reasons why you started on this path in the first place and the rewards that await you at the finish line. By cultivating a positive mindset, you will find it easier to overcome challenges and stay motivated.

Lastly, never underestimate the power of perseverance. Understand that setbacks and failures are part of the journey towards success. Embrace these challenges as opportunities for growth and learning. Remember that every successful person has faced obstacles along the way, and it is their persistence that sets them apart.

In conclusion, staying inspired and focused on the end goal is essential for achieving goals. By defining your goal, breaking it down into smaller tasks, surrounding yourself with inspiration, maintaining a positive mindset, and persevering through setbacks, you will be well-equipped to overcome any obstacles that come your way. So, keep your eye on the prize and never lose sight of your dreams – the power of persistence will unlock your full potential and lead you to achieve greatness.

Overcoming Procrastination and Maintaining Consistency

Introduction:
In our journey towards achieving our goals, one of the biggest obstacles we face is procrastination. We all have experienced it at some point in our lives – delaying tasks, putting off important actions, and allowing distractions to consume our time. However, to unlock our full potential and achieve our goals, it is essential to overcome procrastination and maintain consistency. In this subchapter, we will explore effective strategies and techniques that can help anyone overcome procrastination and stay consistent on their path towards success.

Understanding Procrastination:
Procrastination is often a result of fear, perfectionism, lack of motivation, or feeling overwhelmed. It is crucial to identify the underlying reasons behind our procrastination tendencies. By acknowledging our triggers, we can develop specific strategies to overcome them and regain control over our actions.

Setting Clear Goals:
One of the most effective ways to overcome procrastination is to set clear and achievable goals. When we have a clear vision of what we want to achieve, it becomes easier to stay focused and motivated. Break your goals down into smaller, manageable tasks and create a timeline for each task. This way, you can track your progress and stay accountable.

Creating a Productive Environment:
Our environment significantly impacts our ability to stay

consistent. Minimize distractions by creating a dedicated workspace free from unnecessary interruptions. Utilize tools such as noise-cancelling headphones or website blockers to eliminate distractions. Surround yourself with positive influences and like-minded individuals who can motivate and support you on your journey.

Developing a Routine: Consistency is key when it comes to achieving goals. Establishing a daily routine helps build discipline and creates a structure that minimizes the chances of procrastination. Prioritize important tasks and allocate specific time slots for them in your schedule. By committing to a routine, you train your mind to focus and stay consistent.

Overcoming Procrastination Techniques: There are various techniques that can help overcome procrastination. The Pomodoro Technique, for instance, involves breaking tasks into 25-minute intervals with short breaks in between. This technique helps maintain focus and boosts productivity. Another effective strategy is visualization, where you imagine yourself successfully completing a task, fostering motivation and reducing procrastination tendencies.

Accountability and Support: Find an accountability partner or join a support group with individuals who share similar goals. Regular check-ins and sharing progress can significantly increase motivation and accountability. Celebrate milestones together and learn from each other's experiences and strategies to stay consistent.

Conclusion:
Overcoming procrastination and maintaining consistency are crucial steps towards achieving your goals. By understanding the root causes of procrastination, setting clear goals, creating a productive environment, developing a routine, and utilizing effective techniques, anyone can overcome procrastination tendencies. Remember, persistence and consistency are key ingredients for unlocking your full potential and realizing your dreams. Start today, take small steps, and stay committed to your path of success.

Chapter 7: Overcoming Obstacles and Roadblocks

Dealing with Criticism and Negative Feedback

In the pursuit of our goals, it is inevitable that we will encounter criticism and negative feedback along the way. Whether it comes from peers, mentors, or even our own inner voice, it can be disheartening and demotivating. However, learning how to handle criticism and negative feedback is crucial to maintaining our focus and achieving our goals.

One of the most important things to remember when faced with criticism is to not take it personally. It is easy to let negative comments or feedback affect our self-esteem and hinder our progress. Instead, we should view criticism as an opportunity for growth and improvement. By adopting a growth mindset, we can use criticism as a tool to learn and develop, rather than allowing it to discourage us.

Another key aspect of dealing with criticism is to remain open-minded and receptive. Often, negative feedback provides valuable insights and perspectives that we may not have considered. By listening attentively and considering the validity of the criticism, we can use it to refine our goals and approach. It is important to differentiate between constructive criticism, which aims to help us improve, and destructive criticism, which serves no purpose other than to bring us down. By focusing on constructive criticism and disregarding destructive comments, we can maintain our motivation and continue making progress towards our goals.

Moreover, it is essential to surround ourselves with a supportive network of individuals who believe in our abilities and dreams. Seeking feedback from trusted mentors, friends, or family members can provide us with valuable insights and encouragement. These individuals can offer constructive criticism from a place of genuine care and understanding, which can help us stay on track and navigate any setbacks or challenges.

Lastly, it is crucial to practice self-compassion. When faced with criticism or negative feedback, we should remind ourselves that we are only human and bound to make mistakes. Instead of dwelling on our shortcomings, we should focus on the lessons we can learn from them and use them as stepping stones towards our goals. By practicing self-compassion, we can maintain our resilience and drive, even in the face of adversity.

In conclusion, the journey towards achieving our goals is not without its share of criticism and negative feedback. However, by adopting a growth mindset, remaining open-minded, seeking support from a trusted network, and practicing self-compassion, we can effectively deal with criticism and use it as a catalyst for personal and professional growth. Remember, the power of persistence lies not only in our ability to overcome obstacles but also in our ability to embrace feedback and continuously improve ourselves.

Managing Stress and Overwhelm

In our fast-paced and demanding world, it's easy to feel overwhelmed and stressed. The pressure to achieve goals can often leave us feeling anxious and exhausted. However, it's important to remember that stress is a normal part of life, and it's how we manage it that makes all the difference. In this subchapter, we will explore effective strategies for managing stress and overwhelm, so you can stay focused on achieving your goals.

One of the first steps in managing stress is to identify the sources of your overwhelm. Take a moment to reflect on what is causing you stress and make a list. Is it a heavy workload, personal commitments, or a lack of organization? Understanding the root causes will help you develop a plan to address them effectively.

Once you have identified your stressors, it's crucial to prioritize and delegate tasks. Break down your goals into smaller, manageable steps and focus on one at a time. Remember, you don't have to do it all alone. Learn to delegate tasks to others who can help lighten your load. This will not only reduce your stress but also allow you to focus on the tasks that align with your strengths and skills.

Another powerful technique for managing stress is practicing self-care. Take time for yourself each day to engage in activities that bring you joy and relaxation. Whether it's going for a walk, meditating, or indulging in a hobby, self-care is essential for recharging your mind and body. Additionally, ensure you are getting enough sleep, eating a balanced diet, and exercising regularly. These habits will help you maintain your energy levels and increase your resilience to stress.

Lastly, consider adopting stress management techniques such as deep breathing exercises, mindfulness, and visualization. These practices can help calm your mind, reduce anxiety, and improve your ability to stay focused. Experiment with different techniques and find what works best for you.

Remember, managing stress is an ongoing process. It requires self-awareness, planning, and consistent effort. By implementing these strategies, you will not only reduce stress and overwhelm but also increase your productivity and overall well-being. Stay committed to taking care of yourself, and you will unlock your full potential to achieve your goals.

Turning Setbacks into Opportunities for Growth

Turning Setbacks into Opportunities for Growth

Introduction:

In our pursuit of achieving goals, setbacks are an inevitable part of the journey. They can be frustrating, demoralizing, and sometimes even make us question our abilities. However, setbacks should not be seen as roadblocks but rather as opportunities for growth. In this subchapter, we will explore how setbacks can be turned into stepping stones towards success and how to embrace them as valuable lessons in our quest to achieve our goals.

1.   Embracing   a   Growth   Mindset: The first step in turning setbacks into opportunities for growth is to adopt a growth mindset. Understand that setbacks are not failures but merely temporary obstacles on the path to success. By reframing setbacks as learning experiences, you can start to see them as opportunities for personal development and growth.

2.   Analyzing   the   Setback: When faced with a setback, take the time to analyze the situation objectively. Identify the factors that contributed to the setback and consider what could have been done differently. This analysis will provide valuable insights and equip you with the knowledge to avoid similar setbacks in the future.

3.   Learning   from   Mistakes: Setbacks often arise from mistakes or misjudgments. Instead of dwelling on these mistakes, use them as learning opportunities. Reflect on what went wrong, acknowledge your responsibility, and identify the lessons that can be

learned from the experience. By learning from your mistakes, you can grow stronger and become better equipped to face future challenges.

4. Adjusting and Adapting: Setbacks can also present an opportunity to reassess your goals and strategies. Use the setback as a chance to reflect on your approach and make any necessary adjustments. By adapting to new circumstances and finding alternative solutions, you can turn setbacks into opportunities for innovation and creativity.

5. Building Resilience: One of the most significant benefits of setbacks is the opportunity to develop resilience. The ability to bounce back from setbacks and persevere in the face of adversity is a vital trait for achieving goals. Embrace setbacks as an opportunity to strengthen your resilience and develop the mental toughness required to overcome future challenges.

Conclusion:

While setbacks may seem discouraging, they have the potential to propel us towards greater success. By adopting a growth mindset, learning from mistakes, adapting our strategies, and building resilience, setbacks can be transformed into opportunities for growth. Embrace setbacks as stepping stones on your journey towards achieving your goals, and you will unlock your full potential along the way. Remember, it is not the setbacks themselves that define us, but how we respond to them that truly matters.

Chapter 8: Achieving Long-Term Success

Sustaining Progress and Avoiding Plateaus

One of the most common challenges people face when striving to achieve their goals is the dreaded plateau. It's that frustrating period when progress seems to come to a halt, and it feels like all the effort put into reaching the goal is in vain. However, it's important to remember that plateaus are a natural part of any journey towards success. In this subchapter, we will explore effective strategies to sustain progress and overcome plateaus, ensuring that you stay on track to achieve your goals.

The first step in sustaining progress is to maintain a positive mindset. It's easy to get discouraged when faced with a plateau, but it's crucial to remember that setbacks are temporary. By cultivating a positive attitude, you can approach any obstacle with determination and perseverance. Focus on the progress you've made so far and remind yourself that plateaus are just stepping stones towards greater success.

Another key strategy is to reassess your goals and make necessary adjustments. Sometimes, plateaus occur because the initial goal was set too high or lacked a clear roadmap. Take the time to analyze your progress and identify any areas where you can make improvements. Break down your goals into smaller, manageable tasks, and create a detailed plan to guide you forward. This will not only help you regain momentum but also allow for better tracking of your progress.

Additionally, seeking support from others can be immensely beneficial in overcoming plateaus. Surround yourself with like-minded individuals who share your aspirations and can offer guidance and encouragement. Joining a mastermind group, finding a mentor, or even sharing your journey with a close friend can provide you with the motivation and accountability needed to break through any stagnation.

Lastly, embracing continuous learning and personal growth is essential to sustaining progress. Plateaus can be an opportunity for self-reflection and acquiring new skills or knowledge. Explore different resources, such as books, podcasts, or online courses, that are relevant to your goal. By continually expanding your knowledge and skillset, you can overcome plateaus more effectively and adapt to any challenges that come your way.

Remember, sustaining progress and avoiding plateaus is a continuous process. Embrace the journey, stay persistent, and leverage the power of a positive mindset, goal reassessment, support from others, and continuous learning. By implementing these strategies, you will unlock your full potential and achieve your goals, no matter how challenging they may seem.

Continuing Personal and Professional Development

In today's fast-paced and ever-changing world, the importance of continuing personal and professional development cannot be overemphasized. The journey towards achieving our goals is not a destination but rather a continuous process of growth and learning. It is through this ongoing development that we can unlock our full potential and reach new heights of success.

Personal and professional development encompasses a wide range of activities and strategies aimed at enhancing our skills, knowledge, and attitudes. It involves staying updated with the latest trends and advancements in our respective fields, acquiring new skills, and constantly challenging ourselves to grow. By investing in our personal and professional development, we not only become more confident and competent individuals but also increase our chances of achieving our goals.

One of the key aspects of continuing personal and professional development is setting clear goals. Without a defined target, it becomes challenging to direct our efforts and measure our progress. By setting specific, measurable, achievable, relevant, and time-bound (SMART) goals, we can create a roadmap for our development journey. These goals serve as a guiding light, helping us stay focused and motivated.

Moreover, embracing a growth mindset is crucial for our personal and professional development. Believing in our ability to learn, adapt, and improve empowers us to overcome challenges and setbacks along the way. It allows us to view failure not as an endpoint but as an opportunity to learn and grow. By adopting a growth mindset, we open ourselves up to endless possibilities and pave the way for success.

In addition to setting goals and cultivating a growth mindset, seeking out learning opportunities is vital for our development. This can involve attending workshops, seminars, or conferences, enrolling in courses or certifications, reading books or articles, and seeking guidance from mentors or coaches. By actively seeking new knowledge and experiences, we broaden our horizons and gain valuable insights that can propel us towards our goals.

Continuing personal and professional development is not a one-time event but a lifelong commitment. It requires dedication, perseverance, and a genuine desire to grow. By investing in ourselves, we become better equipped to face the challenges that come our way and seize the opportunities that arise. So, let us embrace the power of persistence and unlock our full potential by continuously pursuing personal and professional growth.

Creating a Legacy of Persistence and Achievement

In the pursuit of our goals and dreams, one of the most valuable attributes we can cultivate is persistence. It is the driving force that propels us forward, even in the face of obstacles and setbacks. This subchapter will explore the power of persistence and provide practical strategies for unlocking your full potential and achieving your goals.

Persistence is the key ingredient that separates those who merely dream from those who actively pursue and accomplish their goals. It is the unwavering determination to overcome any challenges that come our way. When we cultivate persistence, we develop the ability to bounce back from failures and setbacks, learn from them, and keep moving forward. It is this characteristic that sets high achievers apart from the rest.

To create a legacy of persistence and achievement, we must first define our goals clearly. Without a clear vision of what we want to achieve, it becomes challenging to stay motivated and persevere. Take the time to reflect on your aspirations and write them down. This act of committing your goals to paper solidifies your commitment and provides a roadmap for your journey.

Once you have defined your goals, it is important to break them down into actionable steps. By breaking them into smaller, manageable tasks, you will be able to track your progress and stay motivated. Celebrate every small victory along the way, as each step forward brings you closer to your ultimate goal.

Another crucial aspect of persistence is maintaining a positive mindset. Adopting a positive outlook and reframing challenges as opportunities for growth will help you persevere through difficult times. Surround yourself with supportive individuals who encourage and inspire you. Their belief in your abilities will fuel your determination to succeed.

Additionally, it is essential to develop resilience in the face of failures or setbacks. Rather than viewing them as roadblocks, see them as learning experiences. Embrace the lessons they offer, adjust your approach if needed, and keep pushing forward. Remember, it is not about how many times you fall; it is about how many times you get back up.

In conclusion, creating a legacy of persistence and achievement requires a clear vision, actionable steps, a positive mindset, and resilience. By cultivating persistence, you will unlock your full potential and achieve your goals. Remember, success is not an overnight accomplishment, but rather a result of consistent effort and unwavering determination. Stay focused, stay persistent, and leave a lasting legacy of achievement.

Chapter 9: Unlocking Your Full Potential

Embracing Change and Stepping Outside of Comfort Zones

In the journey towards achieving our goals, one of the most crucial aspects is our ability to embrace change and step outside of our comfort zones. It is within these moments of discomfort and uncertainty that true growth and transformation occur. It is through embracing change that we unlock our full potential and pave the way towards accomplishing our aspirations.

Change can be intimidating, often causing feelings of fear and resistance. However, it is important to remember that change is inevitable and necessary for personal and professional development. By staying stagnant and complacent within our comfort zones, we limit our opportunities for growth and innovation. When we resist change, we deny ourselves the chance to explore new possibilities and reach new heights.

Stepping outside of our comfort zones requires courage and resilience. It means pushing past our self-imposed limitations and challenging ourselves to try new things, take risks, and face unfamiliar circumstances. While it may feel uncomfortable at first, it is in these moments of discomfort that we discover our true capabilities and strengths. It is through these experiences that we gain valuable insights and learn to adapt and thrive in an ever-changing world.

To embrace change and step outside of our comfort zones, we must develop a mindset that embraces uncertainty and sees it as an opportunity for growth. We must cultivate a sense of curiosity and openness, allowing ourselves to explore new avenues and perspectives. It is important to realize that failure is a natural part of the learning process. By reframing failure as a stepping stone rather than a setback, we can approach challenges with a growth mindset, enabling us to bounce back stronger and wiser.

In addition, surrounding ourselves with a supportive network of like-minded individuals can greatly aid us in embracing change and stepping outside of our comfort zones. By seeking guidance and encouragement from those who have already navigated similar paths, we gain the confidence and inspiration to take bold leaps towards our goals.

As we embark on our journey towards achieving our goals, let us remember that change is an essential ingredient for success. By embracing change and stepping outside of our comfort zones, we unlock our full potential and open ourselves up to new opportunities and possibilities. So, dare to take the leap, embrace the unknown, and watch as your dreams transform into reality.

Embracing Failure as a Stepping Stone to Success

Failure is often seen as something to be avoided at all costs. It is seen as a setback, a disappointment, and a reflection of our inadequacies. However, what if I told you that failure is not something to fear but rather a necessary stepping stone on the path to success? In this subchapter, we will explore the concept of embracing failure and how it can propel you towards achieving your goals.

It is human nature to want to succeed in everything we do. We set high expectations for ourselves, and when we fall short, it can be disheartening. However, failure should not be viewed as a final outcome but as a valuable learning experience. Each failure brings with it an opportunity to grow, learn, and improve. By understanding this, we can shift our mindset and see failure as a necessary part of the journey towards success.

One of the reasons failure is so important is that it pushes us beyond our comfort zones. When we fail, we are forced to confront our weaknesses and areas for improvement. This self-reflection allows us to develop resilience, determination, and a new perspective on our goals. Failure teaches us to be adaptable and open-minded, as we search for new strategies and approaches to overcome obstacles.

Embracing failure also helps us develop a growth mindset. Instead of viewing failure as a reflection of our abilities, we see it as an opportunity for growth and development. We understand that success is not a linear path but rather a series of ups and downs. With this mindset, we are more likely to take risks, try new things, and persist in the face of adversity.

To embrace failure, it is crucial to reframe your perspective. Start by viewing failure as feedback rather than a personal flaw. Analyze what went wrong and what could be done differently next time. Learn from your mistakes and use them as stepping stones towards success. Remember, every successful person has faced failure at some point. It is how they respond to it that sets them apart.

In conclusion, failure is not something to be feared but rather embraced as a stepping stone to success. By shifting our mindset and viewing failure as an opportunity for growth, we can unlock our full potential and achieve our goals. Embrace failure, learn from it, and let it propel you towards the success you deserve.

Discovering and Utilizing Hidden Talents

In the journey of achieving our goals and unlocking our full potential, one of the most powerful tools we possess is our hidden talents. These talents are unique to each individual, often lying dormant and waiting to be discovered. However, once we tap into these hidden abilities, they can propel us towards our aspirations and help us reach new heights.

The first step in discovering our hidden talents is self-reflection. Take a moment to assess your interests, passions, and curiosities. What activities do you find yourself naturally drawn to? What brings you joy and fulfillment? Sometimes, our hidden talents are closely aligned with our passions, making them easier to identify. By exploring different areas of interest, we can stumble upon talents we never knew we had.

Once you have identified a potential talent, it is crucial to invest time and effort in developing it. Like any skill, hidden talents require practice and honing. Seek opportunities to learn and grow in your chosen area. Take classes, attend workshops, or find a mentor who can guide you along the way. Remember, Rome wasn't built in a day, and neither will your talent. Persistence is key in unleashing its full potential.

Moreover, don't be afraid to step out of your comfort zone. Trying new things and challenging yourself can lead to the discovery of unexpected talents. Embrace the unknown and be open to learning from various experiences. It is through these ventures that we often find hidden gems within ourselves.

Utilizing your hidden talents involves integrating them into your goals and aspirations. Identify ways in which your talents can contribute to your journey. If you have a knack for writing, consider incorporating it into your career or personal projects. If you are a gifted problem solver, find ways to apply this skill to overcome challenges along the way. By leveraging your hidden talents, you not only enhance your chances of success but also find fulfillment in utilizing your unique gifts.

Remember, the power of persistence lies in uncovering and utilizing our hidden talents. They are the secret weapons that can help us achieve our goals and unlock our full potential. Embrace self-reflection, invest time in development, step out of your comfort zone, and integrate your talents into your journey. By doing so, you will discover new depths within yourself and reach heights you never thought possible. So, don't let your hidden talents remain hidden any longer; unleash their power and watch your dreams become a reality.

Chapter 10: The Power of Persistence in Real Life

Inspiring Stories of Individuals Who Overcame Challenges

Inspiring Stories of Individuals Who Overcame Challenges

Introduction:

In our journey to achieve our goals, we often encounter various challenges that make us question our abilities and determination. However, it is crucial to remember that challenges are not roadblocks but opportunities for growth and transformation. In this subchapter, we will explore inspiring stories of individuals who faced seemingly insurmountable obstacles but emerged victorious through their unwavering persistence and determination. These stories will serve as a beacon of hope and motivation for anyone seeking to achieve their goals and unlock their full potential.

1. Sarah's Triumph over Physical Limitations: Sarah, a young woman born with a physical disability, faced numerous challenges throughout her life. Despite being confined to a wheelchair, she refused to let her circumstances define her. With sheer determination and perseverance, Sarah pursued her dreams of becoming a professional artist. Through adaptive techniques and innovative approaches, she overcame her physical limitations and carved a niche for herself in the art world, proving that passion and persistence can conquer any obstacle.

2. John's Journey from Failure to Success: John, a once-struggling entrepreneur, faced multiple setbacks in his business ventures. Bankruptcy, financial crises, and personal losses left him on the brink of giving up. However, he refused to let failure define his future. Through relentless persistence and a willingness to learn from his mistakes, John transformed his failures into valuable lessons. Ultimately, he achieved remarkable success and became an influential figure in his industry. John's story teaches us that setbacks are stepping stones to success if we have the courage to persist and learn from them.

3. Maria's Resilience in the Face of Adversity: Maria, a survivor of a traumatic childhood, battled with self-doubt, low self-esteem, and emotional trauma. However, she refused to let her past define her future. With the help of therapy, self-reflection, and unwavering persistence, Maria rebuilt her life from scratch. She went on to become an advocate for mental health, inspiring countless individuals to overcome their own adversities and embrace their true potential. Maria's story reminds us that our past does not determine our future, and we have the power to rewrite our own narratives.

Conclusion:

These inspiring stories demonstrate the power of persistence and determination in overcoming challenges and achieving our goals. Regardless of the obstacles we face, we can draw inspiration from these individuals who refused to be defeated. By embracing their resilience and adopting their unwavering mindset, we can unlock our full potential and accomplish our dreams. Let these stories inspire you to believe in yourself, persist in the face of adversity, and ultimately achieve your goals.

Applying the Principles of Persistence in Various Fields

Persistence is the key to achieving goals in any field, be it personal, professional, or academic. It is the driving force that keeps us going even when faced with obstacles and setbacks. In this subchapter, we will explore how the principles of persistence can be applied across different areas of life, helping individuals unlock their full potential and achieve their goals.

In the realm of personal development, persistence plays a crucial role in self-improvement. Whether it is adopting healthier habits, developing new skills, or breaking bad habits, persistence is essential. It is about pushing through challenges, staying committed to the process, and maintaining a positive mindset. By applying the principles of persistence, individuals can overcome self-doubt, stay motivated, and ultimately achieve their personal growth goals.

In the professional world, persistence is a characteristic that sets successful individuals apart. It is the ability to persevere in the face of rejection, setbacks, and failures. By consistently putting in the effort and staying focused on their goals, professionals can overcome obstacles and achieve career milestones. Whether it is landing a dream job, starting a business, or climbing the corporate ladder, persistence is the driving force that propels individuals forward.

Academic pursuits also require a great deal of persistence. Students who are persistent in their studies are more likely to excel academically. It involves staying dedicated to learning, even when faced with difficult subjects or challenging assignments. By applying the principles of persistence, students can overcome academic obstacles, improve their grades, and achieve their educational goals.

In summary, persistence is a universal principle that applies to all areas of life. By embracing persistence, individuals can unlock their full potential and achieve their goals. Whether it is personal development, professional success, or academic pursuits, persistence is the driving force that propels individuals forward. It is about staying committed, pushing through challenges, and maintaining a positive mindset. By applying the principles of persistence, individuals can overcome obstacles, achieve their dreams, and live a fulfilling and successful life.

Remember, success is not always immediate, but with persistence, it becomes inevitable. So, embrace the power of persistence and unlock your full potential to achieve your goals.

Lessons from Successful Individuals on Persistence and Goal Achievement

Subchapter: Lessons from Successful Individuals on Persistence and Goal Achievement

Introduction:

In this subchapter, we will delve into the invaluable insights and experiences of successful individuals who have triumphed over obstacles and achieved their goals through unwavering persistence. These individuals have paved the way for countless others seeking to accomplish their dreams, providing us with invaluable lessons and inspiration. By understanding and implementing their strategies, you too can unlock your full potential and achieve your goals.

1. Embrace Failure as a Stepping Stone: Successful individuals understand that failure is not the end but a crucial part of the journey towards success. They view setbacks as opportunities for growth and learning, using them to refine their strategies and move closer to their goals. By embracing failure and persisting despite it, you can cultivate resilience and develop the determination necessary to overcome any obstacle.

2. Set Clear and Specific Goals: One common trait among achievers is their ability to set clear and specific goals. Successful individuals understand the importance of defining their objectives with precision, as this helps them stay focused and motivated. By setting specific goals, you can better measure your progress and adjust your strategies accordingly, increasing your chances of success.

3. Develop a Growth Mindset: Achievement often requires a shift in mindset. Successful individuals embrace a growth mindset, believing that their abilities and intelligence can be developed through dedication and hard work. This mindset enables them to persist in the face of challenges, viewing them as opportunities for growth rather than insurmountable barriers.

4. Cultivate Discipline and Consistency: Persistence demands discipline and consistency. Successful individuals understand the importance of developing daily habits and routines that support their goals. By committing to consistent effort and maintaining discipline, you can make steady progress towards your objectives, even when motivation wanes.

5. Seek Support and Mentorship: No one achieves success alone. Successful individuals recognize the value of seeking support and mentorship from others who have already achieved what they aspire to. By surrounding yourself with a supportive network and seeking guidance from mentors, you can gain valuable insights, receive encouragement, and learn from their experiences.

Conclusion:
Learning from the experiences of successful individuals teaches us that persistence and goal achievement are not reserved for a select few but within reach for anyone willing to put in the effort. By embracing failure, setting clear goals, adopting a growth mindset, cultivating discipline, and seeking support, you can unlock your full potential, overcome challenges, and achieve your goals. The power of persistence lies within each one of us, waiting to be harnessed. So, let us embark on this transformative journey together, and unlock the success we all deserve.

Conclusion: Embracing the Power of Persistence

In this book, "The Power of Persistence: Unlocking Your Full Potential and Achieving Goals," we have delved into the secrets of achieving goals and maximizing our potential. Throughout the chapters, we have explored various strategies, mindsets, and habits that can help anyone, regardless of their background or circumstances, to unlock their full potential and achieve their goals.

Persistence is the key to success in any endeavor. It is the unwavering commitment to keep going, even in the face of challenges and setbacks. It is the refusal to give up on our dreams and aspirations, no matter how difficult the journey may be. By embracing the power of persistence, we can overcome any obstacles that come our way and achieve the extraordinary.

One of the essential lessons we have learned is that failure is not the end; it is merely a stepping stone on the path to success. Many great achievers throughout history have faced multiple failures before reaching their goals. Thomas Edison, for example, failed countless times before finally inventing the electric lightbulb. It is through persistence that they were able to learn from their mistakes, adjust their strategies, and ultimately achieve greatness.

Persistence also requires a growth mindset. We must believe in our ability to grow and improve, even if progress seems slow or non-existent at times. By cultivating a growth mindset, we open ourselves up to new opportunities and possibilities. We become more resilient, adaptable, and capable of overcoming any challenges that come our way.

Additionally, we have explored the power of habits and routines in achieving our goals. By developing positive habits and incorporating them into our daily lives, we create a solid foundation for success. Persistence is not a one-time act but a consistent effort. It is through daily actions and habits that we make progress towards our goals, even if it seems small at first. As the saying goes, "Rome wasn't built in a day."

In conclusion, embracing the power of persistence is the key to unlocking our full potential and achieving our goals. It requires a mindset that sees failure as an opportunity for growth, a commitment to continuous improvement, and the development of positive habits and routines. Remember, success rarely comes overnight, but with persistence, dedication, and unwavering belief in ourselves, we can overcome any obstacle and accomplish extraordinary things. So, let us embrace the power of persistence and embark on a journey towards realizing our true potential.